THE GRASS IS GREENEST WHERE I AM

Love & Light
JOURNAL

This journal belongs to:

_____

Published by:
Conscious Co-op
Boca Raton, FL 33428

ISBN: 978-1-7331728-0-6

Cover and interior design: TheBookCouple.com

When you hold your vision
and take steps toward
your desired outcome,
you can manifest your dream.
All that you want
is waiting to be discovered.

~NOAH CRANE

A Personal Note
from Noah

I have always found journaling to be a useful tool in my transformation and personal growth. Since I am committed to your empowerment, I am excited to bring you this journal to help you on your path. The quotes and questions in this journal are for inspiration and guidance only—use them as you see fit. You can also use this journal as a companion to my book, *The Grass Is Greenest Where I Am*.

I wish you much success on your journey to self-empowerment.

Love,
Noah

To Sab,
Grateful for the love
& Connection ♡
            Love,
               Noah Crane

A TIME FOR CHANGE

No comparison
You are unique.

What makes you unique?

_____

_____

_____

_____

_____

_____

_____

_____

_____

_____

No competition

It interferes with connection.

How do you connect or collaborate with others?

_____

_____

_____

_____

_____

_____

_____

_____

_____

_____

_____

No scarcity

The universe is abundant.

How do you create abundance in your life?

_____

_____

_____

_____

_____

_____

_____

_____

_____

_____

*I live in my own love and light
and share my unique gifts with the world.*

I am blessed and supported
as I go through my journey.

In what ways do I feel blessed and supported?

_____

_____

_____

_____

_____

_____

_____

_____

_____

_____

_____

_____

_____

_____

_____

_____

_____

_____

_____

_____

_____

_____

_____

_____

_____

_____

_____

_____

_____

_____

_____

_____

_____

_____

*It's time to think bigger! Yes, anything is possible
when I believe in myself and my life.*

The grass is greenest where I am because I say so.
I am responsible for my own happiness and creating my own life.

What could I create in my life if I took 100 percent responsibility?

_____

_____

_____

_____

_____

_____

_____

_____

_____

_____

_____

_____

_____

_____

_____

_____

_____

_____

_____

_____

_____

_____

_____

_____

_____

_____

_____

_____

_____

_____

_____

_____

_____

_____

_____

My life didn't change; I changed.
I keep transforming myself to create a life I love.

Soul connection is the key
to an uplifting relationship

Do the people I choose in my life lift my soul and spirit?

_____

_____

_____

_____

_____

_____

_____

_____

_____

_____

_____

_____

_____

_____

_____

_____

I water you, you water me;
we grow together.

When I share my challenges, it gives me a chance to cultivate a deep connection and appreciation for others.

Who in my life helps support me? How can I support others?

_____

_____

_____

_____

_____

_____

_____

_____

_____

_____

_____

_____

_____

_____

_____

No one can do it alone;
together we are "won."

A strong daily commitment to my goals
helps create my dream life.

How can I stay focused on what really matters to me?

_____

_____

_____

_____

_____

_____

_____

_____

_____

_____

_____

_____

_____

_____

_____

_____

As I shift my inner world, I recreate my outer world.
Anything is possible when I believe in Me.

Whatever I put out comes back to me.
When I choose love, I live in love.

What areas of my life would work better if they had more love?

_____

_____

_____

_____

_____

_____

_____

_____

_____

_____

_____

_____

_____

_____

_____

_____

_____

_____

_____

_____

_____

_____

_____

_____

_____

_____

_____

_____

_____

_____

_____

_____

_____

_____

*Creating a world of love, peace, and kindness
is my greatest hope for the future.*

My opinions and beliefs won't change the world,
but my love and connection will.

Are my opinions and beliefs bringing me peace, love, and joy?

_____

_____

_____

_____

_____

_____

_____

_____

_____

_____

_____

_____

_____

_____

_____

_____

_____

_____

_____

_____

_____

_____

_____

_____

_____

_____

_____

_____

_____

_____

_____

_____

_____

True and authentic beauty
lies in our Spirit.

Everything I want is inside me already; my job is to uncover it by peeling back the layers of my life to expose more love and light.

What lights me up, what am I passionate about?

_____

_____

_____

_____

_____

_____

_____

_____

_____

_____

_____

_____

_____

_____

_____

_____

_____

_____

_____

_____

_____

_____

_____

_____

_____

_____

_____

_____

_____

_____

_____

_____

_____

_____

_____

I was born for a reason:
to leave my impact on this world.

I rise by empowering others to rise. Everything I do has a direct connection back to me.

How can I make every situation a win-win?

_____

_____

_____

_____

_____

_____

_____

_____

_____

_____

_____

_____

_____

_____

_____

_____

_____

Love and light shared between us grows an
abundant and beautiful garden of hope.

I Love myself enough to surround myself with people who fill my heart and nurture my soul.

Are the relationships in my life giving me strength, inspiration and hope?

_____

_____

_____

_____

_____

_____

_____

_____

_____

_____

_____

_____

_____

_____

_____

_____

_____

_____

_____

_____

_____

_____

_____

_____

_____

_____

_____

_____

_____

_____

_____

_____

_____

_____

_____

_____

_____

*I don't let "energy-drainers" suck me dry. I choose empowering
connections full of love and light. The right connections
energize me and help me rise higher than I thought I could.*

I have faith that if it is meant to be, it will flow easily like water.
I connect to the flow of life and I am open and flexible to
change direction when needed. I am supported and guided.

What is missing that would create more flow in my life?

_____

_____

_____

_____

_____

_____

_____

_____

_____

_____

_____

_____

_____

_____

_____

_____

If it doesn't flow,
let it go.

*Realizing that feelings can change from one moment
to another, I let them flow and then let go.*

Are my feelings running my life?

_____

_____

_____

_____

_____

_____

_____

_____

_____

_____

_____

_____

_____

_____

_____

Feeling are like circumstances ; I don't define myself by
my circumstances, but rather by my opportunities.

My life is happening exactly how it is supposed to. My job is to shift and change.

What choices can I make today that will bring me closer to my ideal future?

_____

_____

_____

_____

_____

_____

_____

_____

_____

_____

_____

_____

_____

_____

_____

_____

_____

_____

_____

_____

_____

_____

_____

_____

_____

_____

_____

_____

_____

_____

_____

_____

_____

_____

*Make a choice that will create
the future you desire.*

*I am grateful! I am always supported, loved,
and guided by the messengers in my life.*

What messages am I receiving from others to help support my journey?

_____

_____

_____

_____

_____

_____

_____

_____

_____

_____

_____

_____

_____

_____

_____

_____

_I let go of how I think things should be, and I accept
that my challenges are the secret to my growth._

Anything is possible when I believe in myself and in my possibility.

In what areas of my life do I use dis-empowering language which creates a dis-empowering result?

_____

_____

_____

_____

_____

_____

_____

_____

_____

_____

_____

_____

_____

_____

_____

_____

_____

_____

_____

_____

_____

_____

_____

_____

_____

_____

_____

_____

_____

_____

*When I hold my vision and take steps toward my
desired outcome, I can manifest my dream. All
that I want is waiting to be discovered.*

As I help others grow and become free, I am actually growing and freeing myself. We are all mirrors. Your light is my light.

What would I have to give up to create better connections with others in my life?

_____

_____

_____

_____

_____

_____

_____

_____

_____

_____

_____

_____

_____

_____

_____

_____

As I create my life, I trust that everything is here
to teach me and support me on my journey.

Every problem has a solution if I am open to that possibility. I am always supported and loved. There are no mistakes; just lessons.

Can I accept that there are no "mistakes" only learning opportunities?

_____

_____

_____

_____

_____

_____

_____

_____

_____

_____

_____

_____

_____

_____

_____

_____

My mistakes are not failures
unless I fail in consciousness.

Everything I am is mirrored in the world; I must have more compassion and less judgment for myself so that I can have it for others.

Where in my life can I find less judgment and more compassion for myself and others?

_____

_____

_____

_____

_____

_____

_____

_____

_____

_____

_____

_____

_____

_____

_____

_____

When I give compassion and acceptance to others,
I give it to myself as well

When I let go of my old stories, resentments,
fears, and anger, I am left only with love.

How can forgiveness give me happiness, peace and love in my life?

_____

_____

_____

_____

_____

_____

_____

_____

_____

_____

_____

_____

_____

_____

_____

_My commitment to love and compassion will transform
my relationships and shift my life toward wholeness._

Life is multilayered. The question is,
which layer do I choose to live in?

What can I focus on to raise my vibration?

I was meant to grow
and rise to my greatest self.

I am grateful for the people who contribute to me and help lift my soul. I am grateful for those who don't, for they are teaching me self-love.

How can I use rejection as a tool for re-creation?

_____

_____

_____

_____

_____

_____

_____

_____

_____

_____

_____

_____

_____

_____

_____

_____

_____

_____

_____

_____

_____

_____

_____

_____

_____

_____

_____

_____

_____

_____

_____

The universe/God is always communicating with me and guiding me. The question is: Am I listening to its messages?

Every uphill climb has a downward slope, and every low has a high; one cannot exist without the other. I meet myself exactly where I am with love and compassion.

What can open up for me if I accepted myself fully as I am right now?

_____

_____

_____

_____

_____

_____

_____

_____

_____

_____

_____

_____

_____

_____

_____

_____

Actions, rather than feelings,
help me to create the life I love

I am grateful for what is working and for what is not.
Everything is here to help me shift and change.

How can connecting to gratitude create more flow and abundance in my life?

_____

_____

_____

_____

_____

_____

_____

_____

_____

_____

_____

_____

_____

_____

_____

_____

The attitude of gratitude keeps me
present to the miracles in my life.

The solution is always in front of me;
I keep moving toward it.

What am I grateful for that is working well in my life right now?

_____

_____

_____

_____

_____

_____

_____

_____

_____

_____

_____

_____

_____

_____

The flow of gratitude impacts my attitude. Today, I am
grateful for who I am, who I am becoming, and who I will be.

*Fear will freeze me, but love will free me! I must
not let others' fears become my truth.*

What stories do I tell myself that keep me stuck in fear instead of being fully self expressed?

_____

_____

_____

_____

_____

_____

_____

_____

_____

_____

_____

_____

_____

_____

_____

I have faith and trust in myself, so life supports me.
I am meant to grow and rise to my greatest self.

I am stronger and more powerful than my circumstances; I change stressful to grateful.

Can I learn to pause and see the magic of right now?

_____

_____

_____

_____

_____

_____

_____

_____

_____

_____

_____

_____

_____

_____

_____

_____

_In order to love who I am , I must embrace
the experiences that shaped me._

*To get comfortable, it is necessary to get uncomfortable
by stepping into my fears, shifting, and creating change.*

What is one uncomfortable thing I can do today to move me closer to my dreams?

_____

_____

_____

_____

_____

_____

_____

_____

_____

_____

_____

_____

_____

_____

_____

_____

_My actions help me create the tomorrow
I want to wake up in._

I know I deserve to live a life full of love and light. I am responsible to love myself more and believe in me.

Where in my life am I giving my power away to others?

_____

_____

_____

_____

_____

_____

_____

_____

_____

_____

_____

_____

_____

_____

_____

_____

_____

_____

_____

_____

_____

_____

_____

_____

_____

_____

_____

_____

_____

_____

_____

_____

_____

_____

If I can see it in my imagination,
I can manifest it into my reality.

I speak kindly to myself, for what I say becomes
the light or the obstacles on my path.

Where in my life is my limiting belief causing me to think and play small?

_____

_____

_____

_____

_____

_____

_____

_____

_____

_____

_____

_____

_____

_____

_____

_____

_____

_____

_____

_____

_____

_____

_____

_____

_____

_____

_____

_____

_____

_____

_____

_____

_____

I believe in myself and I reach higher than I ever thought I could.
I deserve to be happy, abundant, and fulfilled in this lifetime.

My journey is always here to help me uncover the miracles of my life. Every setback is a chance for self-connection, compassion, re-creation, and love. All is working perfectly in my life and I am grateful.

What areas of my life am I committed to change?

_____

_____

_____

_____

_____

_____

_____

_____

_____

_____

_____

_____

_____

_____

_____

It's time to step into the life that I dream of.

My body is a one-time gift; I take care of my body
so that my body can take care of me

Where can I make more time to nurture my body and soul daily

_____

_____

_____

_____

_____

_____

_____

_____

_____

_____

_____

_____

_____

_____

_____

_____

I make myself the biggest project to work on daily.
I deserve to fill myself with unconditional love and
light. I can only give what is already inside me.

On the roller coaster of life, I would rather be alone than sitting with the wrong person.

What are the qualities most important to me in a partner/ soul-mate?

_____

_____

_____

_____

_____

_____

_____

_____

_____

_____

_____

_____

_____

_____

_____

A true partnership gives my life stability
and a foundation of love to build upon.

*I find peace within myself so I can be
a source of peace in the world.*

How can I fill my cup daily with love and compassion for myself?

_____

_____

_____

_____

_____

_____

_____

_____

_____

_____

_____

_____

_____

_____

_____

I deserve a life full of happiness
and positivity.

I eliminate what is not working
in order to create the life I love.

What can I release from my life that would have it work the way I want?

_____

_____

_____

_____

_____

_____

_____

_____

_____

_____

_____

_____

_____

_____

_____

_____

_Transformation occurs when I am ready
to shift and change._

My words create my world,
and my world is created by my words.

How can I speak to myself in a more empowering way?

_____

_____

_____

_____

_____

_____

_____

_____

_____

_____

_____

_____

_____

_____

_____

_____

_____

_____

_____

_____

_____

_____

_____

_____

_____

_____

_____

_____

_____

_____

_____

_____

_____

_____

My outside world will never give me
my inside peace.

*Being fully self-expressed in my life lets me
paint the world in many different colors.*

How can I create more joy and excitement in my life?

_____

_____

_____

_____

_____

_____

_____

_____

_____

_____

_____

_____

_____

_____

_____

The road to greatness is paved
with opportunities to rise above.

My life is a gift and I treat it that way, as I choose to focus on what is going to be most important at the end.

At the end, what will be most important to me?

_____

_____

_____

_____

_____

_____

_____

_____

_____

_____

_____

_____

_____

_____

_____

_____

_____

_____

_____

_____

_____

_____

_____

_____

_____

_____

_____

_____

_____

_____

_____

I was born in a moment, I will die in a moment. What's most important is what I do with all those moments in between.

Your gifts will touch many hearts and change the world.

How can connecting to my greatness propel me towards the life
I dream about?

_____

_____

_____

_____

_____

_____

_____

_____

_____

_____

_____

_____

_____

_____

_____

_____

I open my heart and mind,
for I am the creator of my life.

YOU ARE GREATER
THAN YOU THINK!

CPSIA information can be obtained
at www.ICGtesting.com
Printed in the USA
FSHW021408280719
60471FS